A LEADER WITH VISION

A Leader With Vision

A Modern Revision of A Message to Garcia for Fire Service Leaders

ERIC SAVICKAS

Convergent Impact, LLC

CONTENTS

First Printing, 2022

Convergent Impact, LLC
6525 Gunpark Drive
Suite 370-164
Boulder, CO 80301
www.convergentimpact.com

PREFACE

I was first introduced to *A Message to Garcia* when I was a junior officer in the Army and attended the Field Artillery Officer's Course at Fort Sill, Oklahoma.

One of my instructors had the book prominently placed on a table in his classroom, and he encouraged us to check it out when we had a chance. I don't remember him telling us about the book or why we should read it. He simply left it up to us to see if it resonated.

It was a small book with large print, originally published in 1899 and only about twenty-five pages long. The author noted the book was written in an hour after dinner one evening and that it had been "translated into all written languages." He also mentioned that it was distributed to the New York Central Railroad employees, the Russian military, and all Japanese government workers.

Later I would learn that these publication claims were disputed. I was disappointed to find out the author also distorted the details surrounding the story of Lieutenant Rowan's mission to Cuba.

Regardless, Hollywood made two movies based on the book. It has appeared at various times on the professional reading list of the

Chairman of the Joint Chiefs of Staff and the lists of the Military Service Chiefs. The phrase "to carry a message to Garcia" used to be popular to describe someone who took initiative and followed through.

But back when I first read it, the book's main point made sense based on my role as an Army company-level officer, especially in the military context. I understood leaders needed people they could trust to do the tasks given and complete the assigned "missions." I knew I wanted to be like Lieutenant Rowan from the story and be the person who could be relied on to "carry the Message to Garcia."

As I advanced in my military career, I often recommended the book to my soldiers. I even gave personally inscribed copies to them when they got promoted to say, "I trust you and believe you are someone who can carry the message to Garcia."

I also reflected on the book's lessons each time I recommended it. And each time, as I learned more and experienced more about leadership, the shine of the book became a bit duller. That's not to say I disagreed with the lessons within it. It just became clear that the author let leaders off the hook and just focused solely on employees, claiming they were the problem.

The saying, "If everyone else is a problem, then you are the problem," comes to mind.

This reboot of "A Message to Garcia" attempts to change the flawed way of thinking that leaders just give orders and team members are simply expected to follow them without question.

I hope this inspires other leaders to recognize that there's a better way.

Eric Savickas
Boulder, Colorado
September, 2022

THE MODERN REVISION

"Leadership, and by extension, followership, is a symbiotic relationship between people. It's not just someone in a position of authority—or with rank on their collar—telling people what to do and expecting them to do it."

A Leader With Vision

War produces many stories. There are stories about overcoming the odds, great sacrifice, heroism, and camaraderie. One story from the Spanish American War has stood out over the years.

During the war, the United States needed to communicate with the various insurgent leaders in Cuba who were fighting for their independence from Spain. Among those was General Calixto Garcia.

President McKinley contacted the War Department and was given the name of Lieutenant Andrew Rowan as the person who could deliver a message to General Garcia.

As the story goes, President McKinley gave the message to Lieutenant Rowan, and with very little instruction or guidance, Rowan accepted the mission and understood what was required and its importance. However, there are conflicting details about how difficult Rowan's journey was, how long it took him, and how much help he had. But that isn't the point.

The point is that President McKinley and Lieutenant Rowan exhibited the best qualities in a truly effective leader-follower relationship. The President wasn't overly directive in what he wanted and didn't micromanage things by telling Rowan *how* he should accomplish the task. Similarly, Rowan didn't complain or ask the President details that were in his ability to solve on his own, like how he was supposed to find General Garcia.

The example of how President McKinley and Lieutenant Rowan handled this small but vital task is the part of the story that should be remembered and retold. It is the example we should look to in developing our own leadership and followership.

Obviously, what happened with President McKinley, Lieutenant Rowan, and General Garcia is a distant memory. Delivering the message to Garcia is only a metaphor at this point. Elbert Hubbard, the author of *A Message to Garcia*, might have you believe it is only about employees "doing the thing" and never questioning the tasks given. While that approach may have worked back in the industrial age, where employers viewed employees as an expendable resource, it certainly doesn't work today.

The attitude that employees simply need to say "Yes, sir" or "Yes, ma'am" and do what they are told is short-sighted, outdated, and frankly, totally ineffective.

Leadership, and by extension, followership, is a symbiotic relationship between people. It's not just someone in a position of authority—or with rank on their collar—telling people what to do and expecting them to do it. Leadership is about inspiring people to work together toward a common goal.

And that's where the "telling people what to do" part misses the mark. Leaders need to express their vision for what needs to be done and why it needs to be done. Employees aren't the problem (or the only problem). The problem is the mindset and approach of their leaders.

The military uses a leadership philosophy called "Mission Command." Mission command-focused leaders develop and articulate a vision of something rather than simply telling people what to do. This means providing purpose, direction, and motivation while empowering team members to decide and take action using their initiative and expertise. These leadership principles work equally well in the fire service as they do in the military.

This type of leadership allows firefighters to take ownership of their tasks and encourages them to think for themselves instead of blindly following orders. As a result, members are more motivated and effective when working individually or as a team.

You may be thinking: "I get it, but sometimes I need my people to just do what I tell them." or even, "There isn't always time to explain the 'why' behind a particular task." The challenge is figuring out what makes you think that and to consider if there is a better way.

When leaders are constantly looking over their firefighters' shoulders, they are less likely to feel empowered to do their best work. But when they give their people clear direction and trust them to do their job, they're more likely to step up and exceed expectations.

This is the difference between leading and micromanaging, and it's something that can have a positive impact on productivity and engagement. Leaders who micromanage their team members are more likely to breed resentment and discontentment than those who take a more hands-off approach. After all, no one likes to feel like they're being constantly monitored and critiqued.

Of course, this doesn't mean that leaders shouldn't supervise or check in with their team during execution. But leading with vision allows members the space to be creative and figure out the most effective way to get tasks done.

As a leader, providing clear intent for any task or requirement is essential. This helps team members understand why it is being conducted and what is expected of them. A well-crafted leader's intent conveys a clear image of the task's purpose, key tasks, and the desired outcome. By articulating the overall reason for a task or requirement, leaders can provide guidance on what needs to be accomplished and help ensure that everyone is on the same page and working toward the same goal without dictating how it should be done.

Picture a fire lieutenant who works hard and wants to be the best leader she can be. She knows her engine company works like a well-oiled machine out on calls, but back in the firehouse, it seems like people are more reactive and often wait to be told what to do. She wishes she didn't have to keep specifically directing tasks and really hates hearing grumbles that most feel like she's a micromanager. The lieutenant knows deep down that's not who she really is, or at least it's not the person she wants to be.

On the second day of a forty-eight-hour set, the lieutenant quickly scans the station and sees one of the firefighters sitting in a recliner watching something on TV. She also looks over to the kitchen and sees the engineer and the other firefighter talking about what they plan on doing when they get off shift. The lieutenant understands that some downtime is good between calls—especially after a long night—but also knows there are requirements that need to be completed and training that should get done.

The lieutenant decides to change things up a bit and applies the concepts of mission command. She remembers it's not about telling people what to do and how to do it, but it's much more effective if she describes the requirement, gives the "why" behind it, and lets them know what the desired end state looks like.

She walks over to the engineer and says, "I've been trying to think about ways to make our quarterly training more effective and impactful, and I don't want it to feel like we're just going through the motions. Can you develop a plan for a water supply training next set that is engaging and gives everyone the level of proficiency to do it if needed on an actual call?"

To the lieutenant's pleasant surprise, after a couple of clarifying questions, the engineer looks at her and says, "I got this!"

A little while later, the engineer returns and gives an update on the task's progress. The lieutenant realizes her folks rarely do that and figured it's because they fear she will just give them something else to do. This time, though, it truly feels like there is more trust, and it also feels like the engineer is happier that he got to figure out how to accomplish the task on his own.

"I want you to know I'm proud of you," the lieutenant said.

Then pausing for a moment, letting her words sink in, she continued speaking.

"I know it seems like I only focus on the negative, like when things don't get done, but you really are doing great work, and I want to let you know I notice."

She could see the pride in her engineer's eyes. The engineer felt valued, and it showed. And the lieutenant admitted to herself that this approach was indeed more effective. It isn't about having rank and just telling people what to do. It's about the relationship.

The benefits of leading with vision are many. When used correctly, it promotes trust and empowers members to take initiative. It also fosters creativity and innovative thinking as team members come up with new ways—when appropriate—to accomplish requirements.

As you know, trust is earned over time through everyday actions and interactions. It can't be gained simply through grand gestures or occasional acts; it must be consistent. This type of leadership creates an environment that fosters trust.

When trust is present, leaders and team members feel confident in each other and will be more effective. But when trust is lacking, team members may be more reluctant to put themselves out there and take initiative. They may also be less likely to cooperate with each other, leading to tension and conflict.

Having the trust to take initiative gives firefighters the confidence to apply their judgment because they know the purpose, key tasks, and desired end state. They act without instructions, when existing instructions no longer fit the situation, or when unforeseen opportunities arise. That way, they can take actions they think will best accomplish the leaders' vision and intent.

Sometimes things don't go as planned, and there are setbacks. Great leaders underwrite these mistakes if there is a "fail forward" mentality. Fail forward means that team members (and the leaders) learn from mistakes and commit to improving the next time. This thinking allows organizations to continue growing, learning, and becoming better overall.

Fire departments don't simply want their members to "do the thing." They want their people to be part of a team, one where leaders and followers work together to accomplish the requirements and meet goals. Sure, someone that can "carry a message to Garcia" is valued and needed, but even more important is the leader who can

Lead with vision!

Lieutenant Andrew Rowan, c.1898
Library of Congress

THE ORIGINAL CLASSIC

"He is wanted in every city, town, and village—in every office, shop, store and factory. The world cries out for such; he is needed, and needed badly—the man who can carry a message to Garcia."

Elbert Hubbard's Apologia

This literary trifle, A Message to Garcia, was written one evening after supper, in a single hour. It was on the Twenty-second of February, Eighteen-Hundred Ninety-nine, Washington's Birthday, and we were just going to press with the March Philistine. The thing leaped hot from my heart, written after a trying day, when I had been endeavoring to train some rather delinquent villagers to abjure the comatose state and get radioactive.

The immediate suggestion, however, came from a little argument over the teacups, when my boy Bert suggested that Rowan was the real hero of the Cuban War. Rowan had gone alone and done the thing - carried the message to Garcia.

It came to me like a flash! Yes, the boy is right, the hero is the man who does his work - who carries the message to Garcia.

I got up from the table, and wrote A Message to Garcia. I thought so little of it that we ran it in the Magazine without a heading. The edition went out, and soon orders began to come for extra copies of the March Philistine, a dozen, fifty, a hundred; and when the American News Company ordered a thousand, I asked one of my helpers which article it was that had stirred up the cosmic dust. "It's the stuff about Garcia." he said.

The next day a telegram came from George H. Daniels, of the New York Central Railroad, thus: "Give price on one hundred thousand Rowan article in pamphlet form - Empire State Express advertisement on back - also how soon can ship."

I replied giving price, and stated we could supply the pamphlets in two years. Our facilities were small and a hundred thousand booklets looked like an awful undertaking.

The result was that I gave Mr. Daniels permission to reprint the article in his own way. He issued it in booklet form in additions of half a million. Two or three of these half-million lots were sent out by Mr. Daniels, and in addition the article was reprinted in over two hundred magazines and newspapers. It had been translated into all written languages.

At the time Mr. Daniels was a distributing was distributing the Message to Garcia, Prince Hilakoff, Director of Russian Railways, was in this country. He was the guest of the New York Central, and made a tour of the country under the personal direction of Mr. Daniels. The Prince saw the little book and was interested in it, more because Mr. Daniels was putting it out in such large numbers, probably, then otherwise.

In any event, when he got home he had the matter translated into Russian, and a copy of the booklet given to every railroad employee in Russia.

Other countries then took it up, and from Russia it passed into Germany, France, Spain, Turkey, Hindustan and China. During the war between Russia and Japan, every Russian soldier who went to the front was given a copy of the Message to Garcia.

The Japanese, finding the booklets in possession of the Russian prisoners, concluded that it must be a good thing and accordingly translated it into Japanese.

And on an order of the Mikado, a copy was given to every man in the employ of the Japanese Government, soldier or civilian.

Over forty million copies of A Message to Garcia have been printed. This is said to be a larger circulation than any other literary venture has ever attained during the lifetime of the author, in all history - thanks to the series of lucky accidents.

E.H.
East Aurora
December 1, 1913

A Message to Garcia

In all this Cuban business there is one man stands out on the horizon of my memory like Mars at perihelion.

When war broke out between Spain and the United States, it was very necessary to communicate quickly with the leader of the Insurgents. Garcia was somewhere in the mountain fastnesses of Cuba - no one knew where. No mail or telegraph could reach him. The President must secure his co-operation, and quickly.

What to do!

Someone said to the President, "There's a fellow by the name of Rowan will find Garcia for you, if anybody can."

Rowan was sent for and given a letter to be delivered to Garcia. How "the fellow by name of Rowan" took the letter, sealed it up in an oil-skin pouch, strapped it over his heart, in four days landed by night off the coast of Cuba from an open boat, disappeared into the jungle, and in three weeks came out on the other side of the island, having traversed a hostile country on foot, and having delivered his letter to Garcia, are things I have no special desire now to tell in detail. The point I wish to make is this: McKinley gave Rowan a letter to be delivered to Garcia; Rowan took the letter and did not ask, "Where is he at?"

By the Eternal! There is a man whose form should be cast in deathless bronze and the statue placed in every college in the land. It is not book-learning young men need, nor instruction about this or that, but a stiffening of the vertebrae which will cause them to be loyal to a trust, to act promptly, concentrate their energies; do the thing - "carry a message to Garcia!"

General Garcia is dead now, but there are other Garcias. No man, who has endeavored to carry out an enterprise where many hands were needed, but has been well-nigh appalled at times by the imbecility of the average man - the inability or unwillingness to concentrate on a thing and do it.

Slipshod assistance, foolish inattention, dowdy indifference, and half-hearted work seem the rule; and no man succeeds, unless by hook or crook, or threat, he forces or bribes other men to assist him; or mayhap, God in His goodness performs a miracle, and sends him an Angel of Light for an assistant.

You, reader, put this matter to a test: You are sitting now in your office—six clerks are within your call. Summon any one and make this request: "Please look in the encyclopedia and make a brief memorandum for me concerning the life of Correggio."

Will the clerk quietly say, "Yes, sir," and go do the task?

On your life, he will not. He will look at you out of a fishy eye, and ask one or more of the following questions:

Who was he?

Which encyclopedia?

Where is the encyclopedia?

Was I hired for that?

Don't you mean Bismarck?

What's the matter with Charlie doing it?

Is he dead?

Is there any hurry?

Shan't I bring you the book and let you look it up yourself?

What do you want to know for?

And I will lay you ten to one that after you have answered the questions, and explained how to find the information, and why you want it, the clerk will go off and get one of the other clerks to help him find Garcia - and then come back and tell you there is no such man. Of course I may lose my bet, but according to the Law of Averages, I will not.

Now if you are wise, you will not bother to explain to your "assistant" that Correggio is indexed under the C's, not in the K's, but you will smile sweetly and say, "Never mind," and go look it up yourself. And this incapacity for independent action, this moral stupidity, this infirmity of the will, this unwillingness to cheerfully catch hold and lift, are the things that put pure socialism so far into the future. If men will not act for themselves, what will they do when the benefit of their effort is for all?

A first mate with knotted club seems necessary; and the dread of getting "the bounce" Saturday night holds many a worker in his place. Advertise for a stenographer, and nine times out of ten who apply can neither spell nor punctuate - and do not think it necessary to.

Can such a one write a letter to Garcia?

"You see that bookkeeper," said the foreman to me in a large factory.

"Yes, what about him?"

"Well, he's a fine accountant, but if I'd send him to town on an errand, he might accomplish the errand all right, and, on the other hand, might stop at four saloons on the way, and when he got to Main Street, would forget what he had been sent for."

Can such a man be entrusted to carry a message to Garcia?

We have recently been hearing much maudlin sympathy expressed for the "downtrodden denizens of the sweatshop" and the "homeless wanderer searching for honest employment," and with it all often go many hard words for the men in power.

Nothing is said about the employer who grows old before his time in a vain attempt to get frowsy ne'er-do-wells to do intelligent work; and his long patient striving with "help" that does nothing but loaf when his back is turned. In every store and factory there is a constant weeding-out process going on. The employer is constantly sending away "help" that have shown their incapacity to further the interests of the business, and others are being taken on. No matter how good times are, this sorting continues, only if times are hard and work is scarce, this sorting is done finer–but out and forever out, the incompetent and unworthy go. It is the survival of the fittest. Self-interest prompts every employer to keep the best–those who can carry a message to Garcia.

I know one man of really brilliant parts who has not the ability to manage a business of his own, and yet who is absolutely worthless to anyone else, because he carries with him constantly the insane suspicion that his employer is oppressing, or intending to oppress, him. He cannot give orders, and he will not receive them. Should a message be given him to take to Garcia, his answer would probably be, "Take it yourself."

Tonight this man walks the streets looking for work, the wind whistling through his threadbare coat. No one who knows him dare employ him, for he is a regular firebrand of discontent. He is impervious to reason, and the only thing that can impress him is the toe of a thick-soled Number Nine boot.

Of course I know that one so morally deformed is no less to be pitied than a physical cripple; but in your pitying, let us drop a tear, too, for the men who are striving to carry on a great enterprise, whose working hours are not limited by the whistle, and whose hair is fast turning white through the struggle to hold the line in dowdy indifference, slipshod imbecility, and the heartless ingratitude which, but for their enterprise, would be both hungry and homeless.

Have I put the matter too strongly? Possibly I have; but when all the world has gone a-slumming I wish to speak a word of sympathy for the man who succeeds–the man who, against great odds, has directed the efforts of others, and, having succeeded, finds there's nothing in it: nothing but bare board and clothes. I have carried a dinner-pail and worked for a day's wages, and I have also been an employer of labor, and I know there is something to be said on both sides. There is no excellence, per se, in poverty; rags are no recommendation; and all employers are not rapacious and high-handed, any more than all poor men are virtuous. My heart goes out to the man who does his work when the "boss" is away, as well as when he is home. And the man who, when given a letter for Garcia, quietly takes the missive, without asking any idiotic questions, and with no lurking intention of chucking it into the nearest sewer, or of doing aught else but deliver it, never gets "laid off," nor has to go on strike for higher wages. Civilization is one long anxious search for just such individuals. Anything such a man asks will be granted; his kind is so rare that no employer can afford to let him go. He is wanted in every city, town, and village–in every office, shop, store and factory. The world cries out for such; he is needed, and needed badly—the man who can

Carry a message to Garcia.

About the Author

Lieutenant Colonel Eric Savickas (US Army, Ret.) is a proven leader, as well as an expert teacher and trainer, with over 25 years of experience as an Army officer, university instructor, and leadership coach.

He formed Convergent Impact to provide military-inspired leadership training to those in the fire service working to make a difference each day. Eric uses his combat-tested leadership experience and practical lessons learned to help individual leaders and their departments develop, grow, and succeed.

Eric is a retired Army Field Artillery Officer who served 22 years on active duty in a variety of leadership and staff positions at the tactical, operational, and strategic levels. Most notably, he commanded multiple artillery units, served on the Joint Staff in the Pentagon, and led the Army ROTC detachment at Eastern Illinois University. Additionally, he served two combat tours in Iraq as part of Operation Iraqi Freedom.

Eric has a Bachelor of Science in Business Administration from Norwich University and a Master of Science in Administration with a concentration in Human Resources from Central Michigan University.

To contact Eric:

www.convergentimpact.com
eric@convergentimpact.com

Convergent Impact, LLC
6525 Gunpark Drive
Suite 370-164
Boulder, CO 80301

www.ingramcontent.com/pod-product-compliance
Lightning Source LLC
Chambersburg PA
CBHW070454130626

46553CB00006B/2406